New Beginnings:
A Sure Foundation

Stan E. DeKoven, Ph.D.

New Beginnings: A Sure Foundation

Stan E. DeKoven, Ph.D.

Copyright © 2015 by Stan E. DeKoven, Ph.D.

Fourth Edition

ISBN 978-1-61529-166-3

Published by:

Vision Publishing
1115 D Street
Ramona, Ca 92065
(760) 789-4700
www.booksbyvision.com

All scripture references are taken from the New American Standard Version of the Bible unless otherwise noted. This book was printed in the United States of America.

Table of Contents

TWO ROADS DIVERGED IN A WOOD, AND I –

I TOOK THE ONE LESS

TRAVELED BY, AND THAT HAS MADE ALL THE DIFFERENCE.

THE ROAD NOT TAKEN, BY ROBERT FROST

Foreword I

I overheard an evangelist relay the following:

"Several years ago I went to preach a three-day crusade in a Western city. The Spirit of God moved in such a great measure that what started as a three-day crusade, lasted for six weeks. During that time, there were several first-time decisions for Christ made daily. The Spirit of revival was tremendous, as many people came into a personal knowledge of our precious Savior, Jesus.

"Approximately one year later I returned to visit the same church. I asked the pastor if I could meet some of the new converts who had been harvested during the crusade. The pastor stated, with some anger and discouragement in his heart, that from the dozens saved, there were only three people that had been planted into the local church. I too was angered and sought the Lord as to why this situation had occurred. I believe the Lord gave me a key to be implemented if we are to stop this tremendous loss of precious souls."

In this church, to no real fault of the local pastor, and much like most American churches, there was no structured follow-up program for new converts. The new Christians were left to their own devices, truly like sheep without a shepherd. Jesus commanded us to preach the gospel and to make disciples. A disciple-making follow-up program would have helped this church to retain the fish, initially gathered into the nets of revival, to build the Kingdom of God.

In this book, one-on-one discipleship in the rudimentary teaching of the Word is presented. Through the proper utilization of Dr. DeKoven's guide, new converts can be adequately grounded in the precious Word of God. Further, as discipler and disciple work and share together, a necessary bond that links people into the local church will be formed. I strongly encourage the usage of this material to ground people in the things of God and to firmly establish their *"New Beginnings."*

Dr. A. L. Gill
World Evangelist and Teacher

Foreword II

Journey

Life is a journey (1 John 2:12-14).

Our natural journey begins with conception; our spiritual journey begins with our new birth in Christ. As with all journeys there are certain principles that, if we adhere to them, will lead us to our destinations. Of course, take a wrong path and you could end up nearly anywhere. Jesus states, "I am the way, the truth and the life. No man comes to the Father but by me." (John 14:6)

There is a journey...there is a way; our relationship with Jesus is a way to our success, and having the Father is our destination (fulfilling our purpose). This book is written to help you, the new student, to learn the very principles necessary to follow Jesus fully, to come to know the Father intimately, and fulfill your destiny.

The Stages

Heaven is a wonderful, eternal byproduct of being born again. However, as wonderful as this is; we are born again to first see then enter the Kingdom of God. The Kingdom includes Heaven, as it is God's rule over everything everywhere, but our Journey is primarily on earth, preparing for Heaven, by seeing and entering the Journey of life to fulfill our Kingdom purpose. John the Apostle, who was closest to Jesus during his ministry in Israel, describes our Journey in three stages; children, young men and fathers (1 John 2:12-14). In brief, childhood is where we all start, and as new believers we need some things (discussed fully in this book). Some manage to know who God is, know that sins are truly forgiven; past, present and future (you belong in God's ever expanding family), and you have those wonderful benefits simply because God loves you just as you are. Thus, similar to a young child, you have a huge learning curve to prepare you for maturity and the place to learn is to be in a loving, nurturing church, where your every effort to grow is rewarded, and your multiple failures and mistakes are lovingly corrected for your benefit. Of course, there is much to learn, and your education will take you to the next stages as young men or women. The timing is up to the Holy Spirit.

Young men and women also have much to learn. Again, John summarizes this as a necessity of becoming strong through the Word of God, (living and written) living in and through you, and having overcome the enemy's attempt to keep you from growing (which is His goal) once you are lost to the Kingdom of Darkness, having become a child of the light.

Many ask; what must I overcome? That is as individual as your unique set of finger prints, but we are covered on the lust of the flesh, the lust of the eyes, and the pride of life (1 John 2:16), more on that later…just know overcoming will happen. God is with you in it, it is normal and natural to have stuff to overcome.

You are not a second class Christian if you have issues, and we all do.

The final stage is Fathers. John summarizes a father as one who knows the Father; His will, His ways, His voice, His calling, etc. In other words, they are mature enough to father children and guide young men and women toward their maturity. Please note, maturity is the goal presented in the Bible as holiness, not flawless perfection. That we will never obtain this side of Heaven, but maturity; yes indeed! Of course, you must choose to take the journey and after being born again (and hopefully soon, if not already), baptized in water and filled with the Holy Spirit.

This book is designed to help you lay a solid, biblical foundation for the early stages of your Christian life. So, get ready, get set, go!

Dr. Stan DeKoven

For more, see *Journey to Wholeness*. Dr. DeKoven. Vision Publishing

Introduction

Several years ago I met with a group of Christians, all of whom had been saved and nurtured within a local church. These people were from various denominational backgrounds and independent churches, all experiencing a sincere desire to develop a closer walk with God.

Our conversation revolved around our early experiences in the Lord. I asked this question: "If you could have had anything different, if anything could have been better for you in the beginning of your relationship with Jesus, what would it have been?"

Though the responses varied, all included the need for a systematic, loving, and consistent training or discipleship program presented by the local church. I found that many, if not a majority of Christians, begin their walk in an almost haphazard manner. There seems to be little vision within the local church for bringing the new Christian to maturity.

Over the ensuing years, I experimented with many materials designed to train new believers in the foundational truths. However, I did not find completeness in much of the material available, and the desire to develop a more comprehensive study began to burn within my heart.

In April 1987, while visiting some dear friends in Slidell, Louisiana, I had the privilege of meeting Dr. Orfilia, a pastor in Slidell. He was beginning a series of studies that he had effectively used in his local church. The material that he developed and taught from, with modification, is the foundation for this book. I am most grateful for his permission to include his research material herein.

As you read and study this material, do so with prayer and an open heart. Complete the homework assignments in obedience to God and share your new insights with others.

This book is meant as a first step[1] subsequent to salvation, in your development of an understanding of the Word of God, enabling you to grow in your knowledge of Him.

If your pastor is teaching from this book, pray specifically that the Lord will anoint and empower him to share the word of truth clearly, as you start your *New Beginnings* journey.

To The Disciple: How to Use This Book

Ideally, this manuscript should be used, either one-on-one or in a small discipleship group. In either case, it is meant to be interactive. After completing each section, dialogue is encouraged between the disciple and the discipler. The New American Standard Version of the Bible has been used. Please take time to look up each scripture and discuss it with your fellow classmates.

Teacher and student should discuss each section upon completion. Questions that encourage discussion between the student and teacher, have been provided. These are only suggestions, and the instructor may use them at his/her discretion.

I hope that you will be able to fully appropriate the information in this book and allow the Holy Spirit to be your guide. By your willing submission to the Lord through the discipleship process, you can be assured that you will grow in Christ, developing a foundation for faith that will be deep and solid. As a new believer or disciple, you will need to be aware of the following five points in order to best utilize the material in this book.

1. Discipleship is not an event, but a process. You must commit yourself to the entire process. Rome was not built in a day, and neither will your knowledge of God's word and basic teachings for life, occur in a day.

2. Read each Scripture completely, think about it, pray over it, and allow the Word of God to sink into your heart. Pray

---

[1] For the next step, see *40 Days to the Promise* by Dr. DeKoven.

every day, specifically for your discipler. He or she will need God's guidance in the process.

3. Answer each question at the end of the chapter in writing. Discuss your answers honestly with your discipler. Our hope is that this will be a start of lifetime journaling.

4. Work towards finding your place of faithful service within the local church.

5. Be willing to change. Change can be very frightening to many people. However, the Lord is transforming us into the image of His own, dear Son, Jesus. That takes time, commitment, trust, love, and patience. In due time, the Lord will help you to become fully grounded in the wonderful things of God, becoming all you already are in Christ.

For The Discipler: How to Use This Book

The training and development of a new convert is an awesome and solemn responsibility. As a discipler, you are being used by God to influence another human being for the sake of the Gospel. This book is designed to help you be more effective in this task.

The following helpful hints will assist you in your vital role with the new believer. Whether in one-on-one discipleship or in small groups (no more than 8-10 recommended) these points are germane.

1. As you utilize the material in this book, remember that the process of growth and change takes time. Those in your care will need small bites at first, which is why this book is broken down into small sections.

2. Meet on a consistent basis. This demonstrates to your new converts the importance you give their growth. If you do not think you can see the process through, do not begin.

3. During each session, you will want to answer general questions, assist with problems, and give biblical guidance. However, you do not have to have all the answers. Part of

our growth comes through the mutual searching for answers from the Word of God.

4. Encourage the development of a prayer journal to record needs and answers to prayer. Prayer should be a vital part of your time together. Remember, your life is a model. Your walk speaks louder than your talk.

5. Look for signs of leadership and let the pastoral staff know if you see potential. You should always be on the lookout for faithful men and women capable of future service.

6. When you minister in this fashion, you are actively involved in the fulfillment of Jesus' Great Commission. Dedication to the task, with joy, will bring positive results for the Kingdom of God.

Chapter I

Sharing Christ

You may wonder why this section would be first in a **basics** book, rather than last as is common. The answer is simple. The new convert's time of greatest opportunity for influencing friends and family for Christ is in the first 90 days after coming to faith in Christ. New converts are filled with zeal and need to learn how to effectively share their newly found faith.

When I was first born again, my pastor had me stand and testify before the church of what Jesus had done for me. I did not know the right words to say, but I knew that Jesus was my friend and that He had loved me.

That experience was the start of my witnessing (sharing my faith) for the Lord. It is vital for every believer to know how to share Christ. We are to win the lost and expand the Kingdom of God here on earth.

Therefore, congratulations on your new beginning in Christ. Share the good news, Jesus has set you free!

Before Jesus left *this* earth, He gave His followers a great task that must be completed before His appearing. He said,

"This gospel of the kingdom shall be preached in the whole world as a testimony to all the nations, and then the end will come." (Matthew 24:14).

A little later, He explained how this must be done. He said,

"Go therefore and make disciples of all the nations, baptizing them in the name of the Father and the Son and the Holy Spirit, teaching them to observe all that I commanded you; and lo, I am with you always, even to the end of the age." (Matthew 28:19-20).

How can we help to complete this tremendous task?

Realize That Winning the Lost Is Our Responsibility

The Great Commission found in the Book of Matthew, was given to all Christians, not just to missionaries or preachers. Jesus told His disciples to teach their disciples to obey all the things He had commanded them. This included the command He had just given them to go and make disciples.

Thus, every Christian should be trained to fulfill the Great Commission until the task is completed. That includes all of us!

Please read Acts 4:31, Acts 8:1, and 8:4. It was not the apostles but ordinary Christians who preached the Word in these occasions.

Claim The Power Of The Holy Spirit

Jesus did not send Christians out to evangelize the world in their own strength. According to Acts 1:4, what did Jesus command the disciples to do before they departed from Jerusalem to begin the work of evangelism?

According to Acts 1:5 and Acts 1:8, what happened to them?

Use Your Relationships With Other People As Bridges To Witness To Them

People are often won to Christ through someone with whom they already have a personal relationship, such as a spouse, son, daughter, parent, sibling, fellow worker, neighbor, or friend. Draw a line from each term below to the scriptural reference that tells how this relationship became a bridge to evangelism.

Brother	I Corinthians 7:16
Household (family) Work	John 1:40-42
Friendship	Mark 5:19
Husband /Wife	Acts 18:2-3
Work	Acts 16:31-34

Share Your Personal Testimony

You can tell what God has done for you. Write out your testimony of becoming born again (why or how) so you can readily share. It should be brief (three to five minutes) and should include these points:

- Your life before you were born again
- How you were born again
- The difference Christ has made in your life

Use God's Word

The Bible is God's Word. When you use it to share the message of Christ, you do so with the authority of God himself; that far surpasses your own opinion.

Here are some verses, known as "The Romans Road," you can use to share the plan of salvation. Get a pocket-sized New Testament or use your smart phone: mark these verses, and carry them with you so you are always ready to win someone to Christ.

Invite Those To Whom You Witness To Pray For Salvation

Prayer as a good deed within itself will not save anyone. But, prayer is a communication to God, expressing our repentance and faith.

Encourage those who confess Christ as savior to be baptized and become part of the church. See Acts 2:41 and Acts 2:47.

Help Send the Gospel

Of course, you cannot preach to the whole world personally. But you can give your time, talent, and treasure to your church to help in its outreach to the community and to the world through missions. Romans 10:13-15 provides God's plan for world evangelism.

Doing The Word

1. Write out your testimony. Share it at your first opportunity.[2]

2. Memorize the Roman Road.

3. Share with the group (or your discipler) how you came to Christ (where, when, why, how).

4. How has your life changed due to your relationship with Christ?

5. Have you shared your testimony? How did you feel?

6. Make a "hit list" of people for whom you will pray and to whom you will witness in order that they might become followers of Jesus.

7. What could you (your church) do to reach your world for Christ?

8. Begin to give regularly for missions to reach those whom you cannot go to personally.

For more, see *Miracle Evangelism:* John Ezekiel. Powerhouse Publishing. And *Strategies for Spiritual Harvest*: Pat Hulsey. Harvestime International.

---

[2] It is recommended that you first practice sharing your testimony with your discipler and then with someone in need with your discipler.

Chapter II

The Godhead and Doctrine of the Trinity

The Bible does not seek to "prove" the existence of God. It simply assumes His existence. Since the human authors of the Bible actually knew God from a personal and sometimes face-to-face interaction, they simply reported what they had both seen and heard.

That God has revealed Himself as a plurality is not just a New Testament concept. The following Scripture is a primary one that clearly shows the triune nature of God: Matthew 3:16. The Old Testament clearly illustrates this concept from the earliest portions and throughout. We can best know God by searching the Scriptures. There, He reveals in the names He uses for Himself; the various aspects of His nature. In the Old Testament, there are three primary names that God has given to reveal His deity.

Elohim, a Hebrew word that means "the strong one," is a plural noun. This word alone indicates that even in the Old Testament times God revealed Himself to men as a singular plurality. God understands that we are not intelligent enough to comprehend the concept of singular plurality, so He uses this name, *Elohim,* or compounds of it, over 2500 times in the Old Testament in order to get His point across.

Jehovah a Hebrew word that means the "self-existent one." Compound forms of this word demonstrate that God is able to meet your every need, such as...

Jehovah Jireh	Genesis 22:13-14	The Lord will provide
Jehovah Rapha	Exodus 15:26	The Lord will heal
Jehovah Nissi	Exodus 17:8-15	The Lord our banner
Jehovah Shalom	Judges 6:24	The Lord our peace
Jehovah Ra'ah	Psalm 23	The Lord our shepherd
Jehovah Tsidkenu	Jeremiah 23:6	Our righteousness
Jehovah Shammah	Ezekiel 48:35	The Lord is present

Adonai is a Hebrew word meaning "master or husband." As master, God has the right to demand our obedience. As husband, He expects our devotion and fidelity. See Luke 6:46-47. He also provides nurture and care in times of need, much as a loving husband does for his beloved wife.

God Is One

The Father is God; the Son is God; the Spirit (Holy Spirit/Holy Ghost, Spirit of the Lord) is God. Confusing...only for most believers since the first century! As confusing as it seems, it is one doctrine or teaching that we accept by faith, based upon the evidence present in the Bible.

The Father is God whom Jesus wanted his disciples, including you and me, to know, and Jesus is the door to know the Father. The Father loves us, and gave us His son for us to take upon himself our sin, and the sin of the whole world! Jesus is God our savior, healer, deliverer, creator and sustainer of all that lives, who sits on the right hand of the throne of God, as our King and intercessor. He prays constantly for us. The Holy Spirit is God who regenerates us, brings our spirit to life, fills us with God's presence and leads us into truth, all for the glory of God and our benefit. They perfectly love each other, are one with each other and have invited us to be a part of their divine family of love.

God's Attributes

Love

God does not merely possess love as an attribute; God *is* love. From that intense love comes His desire for the delight and welfare of mankind. He loves us even when we are not exactly lovable.

God has always shown mankind compassion as an aspect of His incredible love for us. First and foremost, He always desires to show mercy to His creation. His actions epitomize the very nature of love. See Romans 5:8, and I John 4:16.

Eternal

In Scripture, God constantly reveals Himself to us as everlasting, indicating that we can trust Him to be around forever. See Genesis 21:33 and Psalm 90:2.

Immutable

Some people love you when you are good in their eyes and dislike you when you displease them in some way, but it is not so with God. God is not fickle. He is not subject to change in his divine character. He will always love you. He does not change rules in the middle of the game. He will not change His mind about you.

Although times and seasons may change, and although He may carry out His plans differently from person to person, His intent never changes in substance.

Throughout Scripture and throughout human history, this fact is abundantly clear: He does not change in nature. This divine attribute is called immutability. Many places in Scripture indicate His divine immutability. A few of the key verses include: Hebrews 13:8, Malachi 3:6, and Hebrews 6:17.

God Is Spirit

The Book of John indicates that God is an invisible Spirit. He is present with us, even when we do not see Him. This thought may comfort some and disturb others. See John 4:24 and John 1:18.

Omnipotent

God's power is unlimited. There is nothing beyond His capacity to perform. This unlimited power is referred to technically as omnipotence. It should comfort every believer that the God we serve is powerful enough to do whatever needs to be done. Even impossible circumstances are subject to change when the omnipotent God is involved.

The Bible is filled with many different examples of this characteristic of God. Two important Scriptures are found in Job 42:2 and Matthew 19:26.

Omniscient

Have you ever heard of someone referred to as being a "know it all?" Well God really does know all that is knowable. While you as a believer may have things occur in your life that you know nothing about, you can always take comfort in the fact that He knows. Nothing takes Him by surprise! See I John 3:20 and Psalm 147:5.

Omnipresent

When you have done a good job and no one notices, isn't it disappointing? Have you ever wished someone important would walk in just as someone else was taking unfair advantage of you?

In a unique way, God is just like that. Only He is always there to begin with. He has both heard and seen it all. You are not now and you never will be totally alone. Below are a few key scriptures that tell us about God's "everywhere" presence. Hebrews 13:5, Jeremiah 23:23-24, Psalm 139:7-10.

Erroneous Concepts Of God's Nature

There have been many false concepts developed by man about the nature of God. *Pantheism* contends that God has no existence apart from His creation. They say God is impersonal.

In this concept the tree, the rock, and the fire are all God. So too, is the pile of garbage at the local dump or the murderer who is in the act of performing his heinous acts of violence. In contrast is the scriptural view that we serve a living God who sees, hears, chastises, corrects, and teaches mankind. Look at Psalm 94:9-14.

In another false concept, *Deism,* it is believed that God created the visible universe and then abandoned it to itself.

In Scripture, we see that this is definitely not the case. We can see that God sustains and cares for the world and every creature within it. Read Psalm 104:24-30 and Matthew 10:29-31.

The Trinity

It is difficult at times to find human, finite, earthly expressions to fully describe so infinite a concept as the Godhead. This much we know: there is only one God, who has revealed Himself as Father, Son and Holy Spirit. They are separate and distinct personalities. If one would try to incorporate any other concept into the content of Scripture, it would quickly become a mass of confusing and largely useless material.

In Scripture, we see the concept of a compound unity in both the Hebrew and Greek words used for God and referring to Him as one. The concept of a plurality of one begins very early in the Word of God, and it continues through the New Testament. In Genesis 2:24 we see the same word for one God being used to describe the oneness of marriage where two become one.

We see this same word used in reference to people who become closely united for a specific purpose. There is great power in unity. Read Genesis 11:6.

In the New Testament, we see a similar use of the Greek word for one, as a compound unity. We can see it in I Corinthians 3:6-8, in John 17:20-23, and in Galatians 3:27-28.

It is in this way that the Father, Son and Holy Spirit are one. Again, the word *"Elohim"* is the unified plural word used to describe God over 2500 times in the Old Testament. God specifically uses plural pronouns when He refers to Himself in the Scriptures. Read Genesis 1:26.

While they are one, we see clearly in the testimony of Scripture that they are also three separate and distinct personalities. See Matthew 3:16-4:1-6, Matthew 28:19, I Peter 1:2, and II Corinthians 13:14.

To summarize this aspect of God's nature, we would say that there is one God existing eternally and manifesting Himself to us in three distinct persons: **Father, Son,** and **Holy Spirit.**

God has not left us without adequate examples in the testimony of His creation of this incomprehensible aspect of His nature.

One such physical example would be that of water existing as solid, liquid and gas. The gas we call steam. The solid we call ice. The liquid we call water. The other example of a triune being is mankind himself. He is body, soul, and spirit. The three are distinct and able to be separated, at least in our discussion, but they are still part of a single being.

Man himself is created in the image of God. We should not be surprised when we hear such statements as "I was just talking to myself." Just as one part of our being communicates with the other parts of our being without encountering confusion, so it is with the Godhead.

Admittedly, these examples are oversimplifications of what is infinite in nature. However, they serve as patterns of understanding that can help diminish confusion about God. If water can operate in a three-dimensional fashion, why can't its creator? If humans are three-dimensional, why can't their Creator be as well?

Errors To Be Avoided

Historically speaking there are two errors that believers have fallen into from time to time. Some people seek to minimize the oneness of God by promoting the "three-Gods" theory called *tritheism.* Others insist that there is no distinction between Father, Son and Holy Spirit in the Godhead, which is a teaching called Sabellianism or unity.

The Bible teaches that we need to talk to the Father in Jesus' name. He prayed to the Father in the presence of His followers. He said He would send us the Holy Spirit. Failure to recognize the Father and the Son puts a person in danger of falling into the spirit of anti-Christ, as seen in I John 2:22-23.

As believers, we must never minimize the oneness of God to the point where we become *polytheistic,* meaning many Gods, or minimize the triune nature of God to the point we become *unity* oriented and end up denying both the Father and the Son. This is the spirit of the anti-Christ and it is most dangerous.

Doing The Word

Using your concordance or topical reference Bible, find other scriptures that help you understand the trinity of God.

Start a file of references that deal in further depth on the subject of the trinity of God, the various aspects of God's character, the Names of God both in the Old Testament and the New Testament.

Questions For Discussion

1. How is the trinity of God and the triune nature of man similar?

2. What are some of the arguments that are used to refute the trinity of God?

3. What are some of the denominational groups and religious sects that do not accept the trinity of God?

4. Make a list of the strongest arguments to support the trinity concept aside from the scripture.

For more, see *Dynamic Christian Foundations*: Ken Chant. Vision Publishing.

Chapter III

Repentance

When I asked Christ into my life, it was a new beginning for me. Up to this point in my life (I was only 12); I did not have major sin to turn from. However, I knew that I was angry, lonely and rebellious against God, and I needed to change.

When I went to the altar to receive Christ as my Savior, I was asked to confess all of my sins and repent. I did not fully understand the meaning of repentance. I told Jesus everything I could think of that I had done wrong. At that moment, my spirit was brought to life by the Holy Spirit, and my spiritual eyes were opened and I asked Him to forgive and cleanse me. Praise God He did!

This new beginning started me down a marvelous road. You too are on this road, a new life which God has promised is ours when we confess Christ as our Savior and Lord. The first and most important step in that process is turning to Christ.

The foundation of the Christian life begins with repentance. Hebrews 6:1-2 names six foundations upon which we are to build our growth as Christians. These are called "principles of the doctrine of Christ," and repentance comes first.

To help you understand repentance, look for the scriptural answers to these questions.

What Is Repentance?

Repentance is normally translated from the Greek word *metanoia,* which means "a change of mind." However, repentance always leads to a change of life; it is never used for a mere change of intellectual opinions. Thus, we can define repentance as "a change of mind that results in a change of life."

This is illustrated in these scripture references where "change of mind" is substituted for repentance. Matthew 3:8 and Acts 26:20.

The test of true repentance is always a change of life. As we have already seen, John the Baptist commanded his hearers to '

"Therefore bear fruit in keeping with repentance" (Matthew 3:8). Paul preached "...that they should repent and turn to God, performing deeds appropriate to repentance." See Acts 26:20.

Repentance is sometimes confused with either penance or weeping. Penance refers to religious deeds done to absolve sin; it is unscriptural and has nothing to do with repentance. Weeping may accompany the Godly sorrow that leads to repentance as we see in II Corinthians 7:9-10, but the test of repentance is whether it produces a changed life, not whether it produces tears.

Why Is Repentance Foundational?

Repentance is foundational for two reasons:

1. Repentance is necessary for salvation. Acts 3:19-20.

2. Repentance is necessary for Christians who have erred. See James 5:19.

Can A Person Be Born Again Without Repentance?

No. Some Scriptures may seem to promise salvation without repentance for example, John 3:16; Acts 16:31. However, repentance always precedes faith in Christ as Savior, whether it is mentioned or not.

Faith is not merely intellectual belief; it is a personal commitment. Faith is seen in obedience, for we have turned from our own way to God's way. This is illustrated in the following Scriptures: James 2:14 and I John 5:5. The relationship between repentance and faith is summarized in Matthew 21:32 where Jesus speaks to the Pharisees. Please review.

Some people teach that repentance was for another dispensation or age, and that it is no longer required. The Bible does not teach this. This age began with the teaching of Jesus (Luke 16:16), and He taught repentance. Repentance is also commanded repeatedly in Scriptures pertaining to this age.

In addition to the Scriptures already given in this lesson, please look at Acts 17:30. The last book of the Bible, speaking of this Christian age, commands repentance in Revelation 2:5, 16; 3:3 and 3:19.

Doing The Word

1. What are some motives for repentance? Look at the following scriptures and make a list. Luke 13:3, Luke 13:5, Acts 3:19, Romans 2:4, II Corinthians 7:10, Revelation 3:19.

2. Have you repented or turned from sin? Do you as a Christian repent when you realize you have sinned? Does your life show the fruits of repentance?

3. Take time to reflect on your character, that is your attitudes, beliefs, heart motivations, and behavior in light of the Word of God. Do this as you go through your studies. When you find yourself in sin, missing the mark, repent before the Lord and pray with your spiritual leader. This creates accountability and helps you in your Christian walk and ensures your continued growth in the ways of God.

For more, see *40 Days To The Promise*: Dr. Stan DeKoven. Vision Publishing.

Chapter IV

Faith

Shortly after my salvation experience, I compulsively dove into the things of God. I had a hunger to know God and to be a victorious Christian like those I read about in the New Testament. However, after a bit of time, the initial excitement of my new life in Christ began to "wear off." I thought there was something wrong with me!

My pastor related that this was really quite normal for most Christians. He stated that I must learn to live and walk by "faith" in God. Faith in our Lord and trust in Him and in His Word is essential for our spiritual growth. In this section, you will learn what faith is and how to walk in it as a new believer.

Faith is the hand that reaches up to God to receive His blessings. The Word of God declares,

"And without faith it is impossible to please *Him,* for he who comes to God must believe that He is and *that* He is a rewarder of those who seek Him." Hebrews 11:6.

Hebrews 6:1 lists *"faith toward God'* as one of the foundational principles of the doctrine of Christ. Look up the answers in your Bible to these questions about faith.

What Is Faith?

The New American Standard Version gives a good definition of faith in its translation of Hebrews 11:1. "Now faith is the assurance of *things* hoped for, the conviction of things not seen."

The faith that saves is a commitment, not just mental acceptance. John 2:23-24 illustrates the relationship between faith and commitment.

"Now when He was in Jerusalem at the Passover, during the feast, many believed in His name, observing His signs which He was doing. But Jesus, on His part, was not entrusting Himself to them, for He knew all men. "

The Greek word *pisteuo* is translated for "believed" (had faith) and "commit." This is the word Paul used to describe his faith in Christ in II Timothy 1:12.

"For this reason I also suffer these things, but I am not ashamed; for I know whom I have believed and I am convinced that He is able to guard what I have entrusted to Him until that day."

Many people consider themselves believers, and they mentally accept the Bible, but the veracity of their faith is in question.

James 2:14 asks, "What use is it, my brethren, if someone says he has faith but he has no works? Can that faith save him?"

We may call this dead faith, for James 2:17 declares, "Even so faith, if it has no works, is dead, *being* by itself."

In contrast, faith which involves a commitment of our lives and brings salvation may be called *"living faith."* (Romans 1:16-17).

Read Hebrews 11 and see "Faith's Hall of Fame." Notice that every example of faith was a commitment that produced an action by the heroes of faith.

How Do We Receive Faith?

By now, you probably want more faith. Or, maybe you are not a believer at all, but you would like to be. God will never force you to believe, but He offers plenty of reasons for you to believe, if you are willing. But having faith is not hard; it is a gift from God, See Ephesians 2:8-9.

The creation of the world gives everyone enough reasons to believe in God. Faith is not "blind," nor is it a leap in the dark. The Bible assumes the existence of God because the universe, which operates entirely by cause and effect, requires an eternal cause.

So, the Bible begins with God (Genesis 1:1) because His existence is evident to all. See Hebrews 11:3 and Romans 1:19-20.

Why Is Faith Foundational?

As we have seen, faith is an absolute essential in our relationship with God. Here are some of God's blessings which come to us by faith.

Draw a line to the correct scripture reference:

Salvation	Galatians 3:2
Assurance of Salvation	Ephesians 2:8
The Holy Spirit	I Peter 1:5
Answered Prayer	I John 5:10-13
Victorious Living	Mark 11:24, James 1:6-7
Healing	I John 5:4-5
God's Keeping Power	Acts 14:8-10, James 5:14-16

The Word of God brings faith.

"So faith comes from hearing, and hearing by the word of Christ." Romans 10:17.

Miracles inspire faith. According to John 20:31, the "signs" or miracles recorded in the Gospel of John are inspirational; "but these have been written so that you may believe that Jesus is the Christ, the Son of God; and that believing you may have life in His name."

God has given all Christians a "measure of faith" to enable them to exercise the gifts God wants them to have. Romans 12:3-6. It does not mean that all Christians have the same amount of faith. God gives each of us a measure of faith for the gift(s) he wants us to exercise for the benefit of others.

Doing The Word

A true believer is committed to Christ. Are you a believer? If not, God's word promises, *"Believe on the Lord Jesus, and you will be saved, you and your household."* Acts 16:31. NASV

If you are a believer, you must continue to grow in faith in order to grow spiritually.

1. Can you remember a time that you had to exercise your faith in your daily life? Discuss this with your group or teacher.

2. Define faith from a biblical perspective.

3. How can you grow in your faith?

For more, see *Faith Dynamics*: Ken Chant. Vision Publishing.

Chapter V

Baptism

Often in our church, we celebrate baptismal services. What an exciting time we have as we baptize believers in the way Jesus commanded.

When we baptize people, we believe that God the Holy Spirit will move through those doing the baptizing. Frequently, He will manifest the gifts of the Spirit, especially prophecy and word of knowledge. We believe this was a normal occurrence in the First Century Church.

Baptism, as commanded by Jesus, is an outward sign of an inward change in our life. Through it, we identify ourselves with the death, burial and resurrection of Jesus, and celebrate His Spirit living in us.

Let us review the primary Scriptures regarding the truth about baptism in water. Three questions must be answered.

Who Is A Scriptural Candidate For Baptism?

Should infants be baptized, or should only believers be baptized? In Acts 2:38 it states that we must repent before we can be baptized. In Mark 16:16 it tells us that we must believe before we can be baptized. Infants can neither believe nor repent nor need to!. Salvation, which requires both believing and repenting must precede baptism. John 3:36, Acts 16:31, Acts 8:36-37. Baptism in water is only for believers.

What Is The Purpose Of Baptism?

Although salvation comes before baptism, being baptized in Christ, it is incomplete without water baptism. Colossians 2:10-12 shows we are *"complete in him"* by being *"buried with him in baptism."* This speaks primarily of our baptism into Christ, with baptism in water a further act of obedience.

This is to say... we have become complete by dying to our old fleshly nature and accepting the new nature. We demonstrate this through the act of baptism. Baptism is the outward sign of the inner work completed by Christ and now acknowledged and declared by our action. Through our obedience, we demonstrate to the world that we have accepted the fact that the old man of sin has died along with his fleshly nature, having buried our newness of life in Him. In Romans 6:4 it reveals the purpose of baptism. What reason do you find there? We are saved by the answer of a good conscience toward God.

What Is The Right Way To Baptize?

"Baptize" is from the Greek word *baptizo,* which means dip or immerse. Acts 8:38-39 illustrates baptism by immersion.

Only immersion conveys the meaning of baptism. Refer to Romans 6:4.

Doing The Word

1. Were you baptized by immersion? Did you repent of your sins and believe in Christ as your Lord and Savior before you were baptized? Have you been baptized as Jesus commanded?

2. A group of men who had received the baptism of John the Baptist learned the truth about Jesus, and they were re-baptized in Acts 19:1-5. Shouldn't you do the same? This passage both justifies and requires the rebaptism of those baptized into cults such as Jehovah's Witness and Mormonism. If you have been scripturally baptized, you can remember as long as you live that it means you are dead to sin and alive to God.

3. Describe your experience, when you were baptized.

For more, see *Clothed with Power:* Ken Chant. Vision Publishing.

Chapter VI

The Infilling of the Holy Spirit

When I was seventeen, a new hunger for the things of God began to develop in me. I hungered for something new and fresh, to give me power to live the Christian life.

I was raised in a church that did not believe in what the Bible calls the Baptism or the infilling of the Holy Spirit. They even taught us that the gifts of the Spirit, especially speaking in tongues, were not for today. How terribly mistaken they were. Nonetheless, in my exuberance for God, I began to search the Scriptures and pray for this new work of grace in me.

You see, in reality, when I accepted Christ as Savior, I had all of God that I could have. I was a new creation, seated in heavenly places with Christ, an adopted son with all the rights and privileges of my adoption. However, God did not have all of me.

The Lord led me to a fellowship of believers that He used to lead me into this marvelous experience. I received the fullness of His Spirit, spoke in tongues and experienced a new power (Dunamis) for witness and ministry. This experience, which is available for all believers, is vital for our growth in God.

The baptism in the Holy Spirit is so important that God's plan for world evangelism had to wait for it.

"but you will receive power when the Holy Spirit has come upon you; and you shall be My witnesses both in Jerusalem, and in all Judea and Samaria, and even to the remotest part of the earth." Acts 1:8.

The baptism in the Holy Spirit is one of the "baptisms" in Hebrews 6:1-2, which lists some foundational principles of the doctrine of

Christ. Let us find out more about it. It will be helpful if we ask the following questions:

Who Is The Holy Spirit?

The Holy Spirit is God in the form of Spirit. In John 4:24, Jesus says, *"God is spirit."* The Holy Spirit is a person, not an impersonal force. Jesus spoke of the Holy Spirit as a person when He used the personal pronouns "he" and "him" to refer to Holy Spirit in John 16:7-15.

What Is The Baptism In The Holy Spirit?

Baptism, as mentioned in chapter 5, is from a Greek word meaning immersion. Baptism in Holy Spirit is immersion in Holy Spirit. Note these other expressions equivalent to "Baptism in the Holy Spirit:" *'clothed with power'* Luke 24:49; *'receive'* Acts 8:17; 19:2; *'fell upon'* Acts 10:44; *'the gift of'* Acts 2:38; 10:45; *'poured out upon'* Acts 10:45; *'came on them'* Acts 19:6.

Is The Baptism In The Holy Spirit The Same As Salvation?

People are not always automatically baptized in Holy Spirit when they are born-again by Holy Spirit. Every Christian who is born-again is indwelt by Holy Spirit, John 3:1-8, but the Baptism in Holy Spirit is subsequent to and separate from the indwelling of Holy Spirit at salvation for most believers today.

Romans 8:9, "However, you are not in the flesh but in the Spirit, if indeed the Spirit of God dwells in you. But if anyone does not have the Spirit of Christ, he does not belong to Him. "

Remember, in Acts 1:4-8, Jesus commanded the disciples to be baptized in Holy Spirit, even though He had already breathed on them and said, *"Receive the Holy Spirit"* (John 20:22). The same can be seen in the case of some Samaritans in Acts 8:14-16.

These Samaritans, having believed and been baptized in Jesus' name, had been born-again of the indwelling Spirit of God, yet they did not experience the baptism in the Spirit until they were taught and were prayed over.

The Greek expression used for "receive the Holy Spirit" means to actively take or grasp. A Christian may be indwelt by the Holy Spirit without actively receiving the Spirit. When we are saved, the Holy Spirit is in us; when we are baptized in the Holy Spirit, He fills and comes upon us, with power to be God's witnesses as we see in Acts 1:8.

What Is The Normative Immediate Evidence Of The Baptism In The Holy Spirit?

There are four instances recorded in the Book of Acts when people received the Baptism in the Holy Spirit. Let us look at these scriptures for an answer to this question. Acts 2:1-4, Acts 8:18, Acts 10:44-46, and Acts 19:6.

In each of these instances, observers could see outward results of the Baptism in the Holy Spirit. These results included exalting God, prophesying, and speaking in tongues, with speaking in tongues being the most common. Therefore, speaking in tongues is the most predominate initial evidence of the Baptism in the Holy Spirit.

How Can You Receive The Baptism In The Holy Spirit?

Draw a line to the scripture reference for each of these steps.

You must be a Christian	Acts 2:4
Be in obedience to God	Acts 5:32
Ask for the Holy Spirit	John 7:39
Submit to laying on of hands	Acts 19:6
Believe God to give the Spirit	John 14:17
Speak in other tongues as	Luke 11:13

Doing The Word

1. Have you received the Holy Spirit since you believed? Acts 19:6. Discuss. If not, ask your Pastor or another Spirit-filled Christian to pray with you and lay hands on you for the baptism with the Holy Spirit.

2. After receiving the Baptism of the Holy Spirit[3], what has changed in your life?

3. Who is the Holy Spirit?

4. What is the normative immediate evidence of Holy Spirit baptism?

---

[3] For more, see *Clothed with Power*: Ken Chant. Vision Publishing.

Chapter VII

The Fruit of the Holy Spirit

"But the fruit of the Spirit is love, joy, peace, patience, kindness, goodness, faithfulness, gentleness, self-control; against such things there is no law" Galatians 5:22-23.

What a glorious listing of virtues we find in the Apostle Paul's letter to the church at Galatia. Who could reasonably debate the value of any one of the aforementioned fruit of the Spirit? A great confusion is possible for new believers in understanding the difference between the fruit of the Spirit and a doctrine of works or legalistic behavior. New believers are frequently drawn into groups that place an unhealthy emphasis on works in order to become or stay saved.

The fruit of the Spirit is produced by the Holy Spirit within the life of every believer who in partnership with God's Spirit properly cultivates such fruit. There is however, a counterfeit to the fruit of the Spirit, and that counterfeit is revealed in Galatians 3:1-5 where Paul chastises those who think salvation depends upon following a set of rituals. See also Colossians 2:16-23.

It is often true, both in the world and in the church, that we give praise to the powerful personalities rather than the good and noble in character. That is to say, we are greatly impressed with great performances. Could it be that our current cultural standards for greatness may not in fact be in harmony with God's standards for greatness?

For example, many of America's greatest sports heroes in recent history have turned out in fact, to be persons of very dubious character. Drug-addicted and spouse-abusing men and women have been idolized by the media and even by the church.

God, in fact, has considerably different standards for measuring a Christian's greatness than does our society or culture. The Lord is more interested in character than charisma, in godliness than greatness, in showing love rather than impressing people with religious accomplishments.

Jesus commented on the unhealthy preoccupation with size and statistics many times throughout his teaching ministry. One very clear and prominent example of this is found in Mark 12:41-44.

God certainly looks upon the heart, while we as natural human beings have a real tendency to focus on the externals of life and its issues. What is God really after? What are His true standards for greatness, growth, and maturity? Scripture is not silent on this matter!

Scripture places far greater value on the fruit of the Spirit than it does external displays of holiness or large numbers. Even great feats of supernatural power are secondary to a transformed life. See Matthew 7:21-28.

John 15:4, "Abide in Me, and I in you. As the branch cannot bear fruit of itself unless it abides in the vine, so neither *can* you unless you abide in Me."

Again in John 15:7, "If you abide in Me, and My words abide in you, ask whatever you wish, and it will be done for you."

In Psalm 1:1-3, David states, "How blessed is the man who does not walk in the counsel of the wicked, Nor stand in the path of sinners, Nor sit in the seat of scoffers! But his delight is in the law of the LORD, And in His law he meditates day and night.

He will be like a tree *firmly* planted by streams of water, Which yields its fruit in its season And its leaf does not wither; And in whatever he does, he prospers. "

Fundamentally then, the fruit of the Holy Spirit would be that virtue which is produced in our lives by the Spirit of God as we cooperate with Him in cultivating that virtue.

Since cultivation of the fruit of the Spirit revolves around the Word of God, it would assist us greatly to look briefly at God's Word as it relates to each of the differing aspects of the fruit of the Spirit.

Love

Love involves our relationship with others and with God. It *is* the fruit manifested as the rest of the listed attributes. It endures!

Love Of God

I John 4:7-11, "Beloved, let us love one another, for love is from God; and everyone who loves is born of God and knows God. The one who does not love does not know God, for God is love. By this the love of God was manifested in us, that God has sent His only begotten Son into the world so that we might live through Him. In this is love, not that we loved God, but that He loved us and sent His Son *to be* the propitiation for our sins, Beloved, if God so loved us, we also ought to love one another."

By this passage and others like it, we can readily see how God's love progressively moves from love of one's self, through God's love of us, to the love of God, to the loving of others created in His image. It is made readily apparent that our ability to love in all three realms has its origin in the love of God for us.

Love Of Others

The love of others is a primary expression of God's Spirit in our lives. Its importance is made clear by the words of Jesus Himself. See Matthew 5:43-45.

To the Pharisees, *neighbor* was a narrowly defined term. Neighbors were to be loved, but enemies could be hated. Jesus expanded the definition of neighbor to include enemies. See especially the parable of the good Samaritan. See Luke 10:25-37.

Love Of Self

When asked which is the greater commandment, in Matthew 22:37, what was Jesus' response?

It is apparent from our Lord's response that one must have a love of oneself as a foundation for loving others. We can truly love ourselves because God loves us.

In I John chapter 4:19 we find *"we love him because he first loved us. "* God both has loved us and continues to love us even when we are unlovely, with all of our imperfections and shortcomings. Thus, we can be at liberty to love ourselves, even as God does, and subsequently we are free to love others.

Joy

Nehemiah 8:10, "Then he said to them, "Go, eat of the fat, drink of the sweet, and send portions to him who has nothing prepared; for this day is holy to our Lord. Do not be grieved, for the joy of the LORD is your strength.""

Romans 14:17, "for the kingdom of God is not eating and drinking, but righteousness and peace and joy in the Holy Spirit."

Romans 15:13, "Now may the God of hope fill you with all joy and peace in believing, so that you will abound in hope by the power of the Holy Spirit."

Joy is the positive feeling of the whole man that the will of the Lord is being done. Such joy was demonstrated by our Lord Jesus Christ when He suffered and died for us. It was in fact the chief motivating factor and the apparent source of strength for His vicarious suffering. See Hebrews 12:2.

Peace

For an exercise in understanding God's commitment to bringing peace to our lives, just take a look at how many times this particular fruit of the Spirit is communicated to the saints by the apostles in the opening and closing statements of the New Testament epistles.

James and I John are the only New Testament epistles that neither end or begin with a strong reference to blessing the saints with the peace that comes from God to the Body of Christ. Of particular interest is a characteristic of peace that is non-typical to today's culture. Read Romans 6:20 and Hebrews 13:20-21.

Peace is not passive. It is associated directly with the very resurrection of Christ. It resurrects the life of God within us, and it crushes the power of Satan without as seen in Romans16:20.

Another Scripture of interest on the peace of God, presenting an important aspect of the fruit of the Spirit is Romans 8:6, "For the mind set on the flesh is death, but the mind set on the Spirit is life and peace." We make the choice of what or who we set our mind on!

Long-Suffering

Long-suffering can be defined as long and patient endurance of offense. Scripture speaks of this great virtue in several passages, and through our review of them we can learn of this work of the Spirit in our lives. In the New American Standard Version of the Bible the word for Long-suffering is translated *patience.* Look at I Timothy 1:16, II Timothy 3:10, II Corinthians 6:6, Colossians 1:11, Colossians 3:12, and II Peter 3:15.

Gentleness

Gentleness is that which keeps us from being unkind or harsh to others. To be gentle is to be equitable and fair, not insisting on keeping the letter of the law, and before judging looking objectively and reasonably at the facts of the situation. Some versions of scripture use the word *kindness* instead of *gentleness.*

Gentleness avoids causing pain whenever possible. Gentleness towards others is an attribute of great grace needed in the Body of Christ.

Ephesians 2:7, "so that in the ages to come He might show the surpassing riches of His grace in kindness toward us in Christ Jesus."

Colossians 2:12, "having been buried with Him in baptism, in which you were also raised up with Him through faith in the working of God, who raised Him from the dead."

II Peter 1:7 "and in your godliness, brotherly kindness, and in *your* brotherly kindness, love."

Goodness

Goodness is love in action. It not only desires for the welfare of others but also acts to see that welfare is realized. Being good is more than being righteous. The Bible makes a definite difference between the two in Romans 5:7, "For one will hardly die for a righteous man; though perhaps for the good man someone would dare even to die."

A righteous person could evict a widow for not paying her rent, and would have the legal right to do so. Righteousness would keep the letter of the law, but goodness would assist her in her troubles.

Faith

Faith emphasizes our relationship with God. When it refers to our belief in Christ, *faith* means "a firm persuasion." However, in Galatians 5:22, faith refers to "faithfulness, fidelity, or trustworthiness." This faith is that characteristic which causes one to be true to his promise and faithful to his task. Matthew 25:21.

Meekness

Meekness is not weakness. It is not the opposite of courage, but it is strength under control. It is a spirit of humility that refuses to let pride rule one's life. Meekness means that we have the mind of Christ allowing Jesus to control our lives. The meek person does not throw his weight around. Meekness is actually the proper use of authority and power. Christ is our example of meekness as we see in Philippians 2:5.

Self-Control

To most of us the word *temperance* conveys the idea of abstinence from alcoholic beverages, but as a part of the fruit of the Spirit it refers to self-control. It is that virtue found in the life of one who masters his desires and passions, especially in regard to sensual appetites. Perhaps the best illustration of self-control is seen in Christ as he faced the cross in the Garden of Gethsemane.

Matthew 26:39, "And He went a little beyond *them,* and fell on His face and prayed, saying, "My Father, if it is possible, let this cup pass from Me; yet not as I will, but as You will."

In summary, the fruit of the Spirit is singular. It is like a pie that has been divided into nine pieces. Each one of the characteristics is required if there is to be a whole. The list of the fruit of the Spirit ends with *"against such there is no law."* The Law could not produce such fruit. Only the Holy Spirit can lift us out of legalistic law-keeping into fruitful discipleship.

Doing The Word

1. List and define the fruit of the Holy Spirit.

2. Examine how the fruit, of the Holy Spirit, is in operation in your life.

3. What part of the fruit do you struggle with the most?

4. Ask God to help you to surrender to the work of the Holy Spirit so that His fruit may be in operation in your life and ministry at all times.

For more, see *Fruit, More Fruit, Much Fruit*: Eugene Smith. Vision Publishing

Chapter VIII

Praise and Worship

According to many theologies, before Satan was cast down from heaven, he was the angel Lucifer, leader of praise and worship before God. However, because of his rebellion, we have become God's chosen replacements to bring praise and worship to the King of Kings and Lord of Lords. Whether Satan was a musician or not is inconsequential... music is an important medium for communication.

To praise is to express approval or admiration. Praise is one form of worship. To worship is to bow in reverence and submission.

The Essential Worship

Romans 12:1 reveals that we express true worship by offering our bodies in obedience as a living and holy sacrifice. To worship is to bow our wills in obedience to God as well as to adore God with our praise.

It is most important that we be in a church that believes in a biblical pattern of worship. Jesus said, "God is spirit, and those who worship Him must worship in spirit and truth."

Truth is the Word of God. Spirit refers to the Holy Spirit, but also speaks of our heartfelt expression. Both are needed to be true worshipers.

How Do We Begin To Praise The Lord?

Psalm 100:4 says, "Enter His gates with thanksgiving, *And* His courts with praise. Give thanks to Him, bless His name."

Each day we have a fresh opportunity to acknowledge the wonderful presence of God in our lives. As we open our mouths to give thanks, we "open the gates" to his presence.

What Expressions Of Praise Are There?

As we enter into praise and worship, two things begin to occur. First, we minister to the Lord. He in turn ministers to us. Praise and worship of our precious Lord (Trinity) flows naturally from a grateful heart; grateful for our salvation, healing, wholeness and grace that the Lord has given to us. Thus, God has provided many expressions of praise; all for our blessing.

Lifting your hands "Therefore I want the men in every place to pray, lifting up holy hands, without wrath and dissension, "I Timothy 2:8, Psalm 63:4.

Speaking 'Through Him then, let us continually offer up a sacrifice of praise to God, that is, the fruit of lips that give thanks to His name, " Hebrews 13:15, Revelation 19:1-6.

Singing "And do not get drunk with wine, for that is dissipation, but be filled with the Spirit, speaking to one another in psalms and hymns and spiritual songs, singing and making melody with your heart to the Lord;" Ephesians 5:18-

19, Colossians 3:16.

Playing musical instruments and dancing "Praise Him with trumpet sound; Praise Him with harp and lyre. Praise Him with timbrel and dancing; Praise Him with stringed instruments and pipe. Praise Him with loud cymbals; Praise Him with resounding cymbals." Psalms 150:3-5, Revelation 14:2.

Speaking in unison with one another "And when they heard *this,* they lifted their voices to God with one and said, "Lord, it is You who made the heaven and the earth and the sea, and all that is in them," Acts 4:2.

When Should We Praise And Worship?

In all things give thanks. Praise should continually be upon our lips. We should praise the Lord when we feel gratitude to God, but also when we feel down and depressed. Isaiah 6:1 says that the Lord will give us a *"garment of praise for the spirit of heaviness."*

We are able to experience the very presence of God as we praise Him. Colossians 3:17 says, "Whatever you do in word or deed, *do* all in the name of the Lord Jesus, giving thanks through Him to God the Father" Verse 23 adds, "Whatever you do, do your work heartily, as for the Lord rather than for men,"

Joy is intensified in our lives as we worship God by doing only those things that can be done in His name and by doing all with a heart to honor and glorify Him. A life of worship and praise is a life of great joy and peace.

Where Should Praise And Worship Occur?

At home, in church, and with friends; spontaneously at work; we are to praise him at all times! "Let everything that has breath praise the Lord." Psalm 150:6.

Doing The Word

1. Think of three things that you are thankful for and discuss them.

2. Define praise and worship. Discuss their similarities and differences.

3. Do you praise and worship each day, or only on Sunday? Make a commitment to be a praiser and worshiper, not a murmurer and a complainer.

For more, see *Redemption: The Foundation of Worship*: Dr. Michael Elliott. Vision Publishing

Chapter IX

Prayer

In Jesus' life, prayer held a prominent place. Before Jesus chose His disciples, before facing the cross, and many times in between, He would steal away to be alone with His Father.

These were times of intense communication with God the Father. If Jesus needed to get away and pray, how much more do we?

The apostles, after the resurrection of Christ, continued to emphasize prayer as an important part of the development and maintenance of spiritual vitality. Let us look more closely at some of the key aspects of prayer.

What Is Prayer?

Prayer has been called the key to heaven. It is communication with God. Communication should be a vital part of any relationship, especially our relationship with God. But what is prayer anyway?

In Matthew 7:7-8, we find that prayer is, "Ask, and it will be given to you; seek, and you will find; knock, and it will be opened to you. For everyone who asks receives, and he who seeks finds, and to him who knocks it will be opened."

Simply, it is asking, seeking, knocking and learning to listen when God replies.

Why Pray?

In Luke 18:1, we read that Jesus told His disciples a parable to show them that they should always pray and not give up. Further, Paul tells us to *"pray without ceasing"*. I Thessalonians 5:17. So, we see that the Lord does not suggest that we pray, but He commands us to pray.

There is great power in prayer, especially the prayer of agreement. In Matthew 18:19, we read, "Again I say to you, that if two of you agree on earth about anything that they may ask, it shall be done for them by My Father who is in heaven. "

How Do We Pray?

The disciples asked this same question of Jesus, who was a man of prayer. In Matthew 6:9-13, we find a pattern for prayer called the "Our Father."

Matthew 6:9-13, "Pray, then, in this way: 'Our Father who is in heaven, Hallowed be Your name. Your kingdom come. Your will be done, On earth as it is in heaven. Give us this day our daily bread. And forgive us our debts, as we also have forgiven our debtors. And do not lead us into temptation, but deliver us from evil. For Yours is the kingdom and the power and the glory forever. Amen.'"

In very simplified terms, this pattern teaches us to do the following:

1. Acknowledge the greatness of God and give the praise due Him.

2. Seek His will to be done in our lives and in this world.

3. Make petition or request for our basic needs. (We are to ask even though God already knows.)

4. Acknowledge that we need forgiveness from God and for our fellow man. A lack of forgiveness can hinder our prayers (Psalm 66:18).

5. Seek assistance in resisting temptation and battling the devil.

6. Praise God for His provision and many blessings.

Further, our prayer must be *"in faith."* Matthew 21:22 says, "And all things you ask in prayer, believing, you will receive" Our faith grows as we read and do the Word of God. See Romans 10:17. Faith pleases God. See Hebrews 11:6.

By faith we can come boldly before God (see Hebrews 4:16).

Where To Pray?

When we were born-again, God gave us the right to have direct access to Him. Therefore, we can pray anywhere at any time. Acts 12:5 states that, "So Peter was kept in the prison, but prayer for him was being made fervently by the church to God. " Peter prayed on a rooftop in Acts 10:9. Jesus prayed in the desert, Luke 4:1 and in a solitary place, Mark 1:35. Paul and Silas prayed in prison, Acts 16:25. We can and should pray anywhere and everywhere.

Hindrances To Prayer

There may be times in your Christian experience when it feels as though God is far from you. As it were, the "skies are brass." However, God is there and does still hear and answer. Though God is always near, we can hinder God's moving on our behalf. We have already looked at forgiveness and faith above, which are necessary ingredients to effective prayer.

Further, I Peter 3:7 says,

"You husbands in the same way, live with *your wives* in an understanding way, as with someone weaker, since she is a woman; and show her honor as a fellow heir of the grace of life, so that your prayers will not be hindered."

Keeping a good relationship with your spouse is very important. Read more in Chapter XVII.

Does God Answer All Prayer?

This is a question that most Christians ask. Does God really care enough about me to answer my specific prayers? The answer is yes.

"If you abide in Me, and My words abide in you, ask whatever you wish, and it will be done for you," John 15:7.

As we daily walk with the Lord, by faith in the fact of our salvation, and as we abide in and hold onto the Word of God, we can be assured of God's answer to our prayers. However, the answer is not always yes or no. It can also be wait. Waiting on God builds Christian character.

Prayer is a vital exercise that is as important in one's life with God as communication is in one's life with a spouse. We must practice it many times a day and make it a priority for life. Remember, I Thessalonians 5:17 instructs us to pray without ceasing.

Doing The Word

1. Discuss a specific answer to a specific prayer from your experience.

2. Respond to the questions, from your experience;

   a. Why pray?

   b. Where to pray?

   c. Does God answer all prayers?

3. Begin a "prayer journal" of things being prayed for and answers received. Also, write down "nuggets" from the Holy Spirit that are revealed to you in prayer.

4. Covenant with the group to pray specifically for them, and set aside a time daily for this service to God.

For more, see *Prayer Power*: Dr. Stan DeKoven and Dr. John Delgado. Vision Publishing.

Chapter X

The Word of God

What Is The Word Of God?

In the book *Fresh Manna*, there are actually three Greek words for word; Logos, Graphe, Rhema. As previously discussed; Jesus is The Living Word, eternally facing the Father and Holy Spirit. In this chapter we review the importance of the written word. The people of God should read, study, and cherish the Word of God. It is God's communication with His people. The Word of God reveals Jesus, the Word made flesh in John 1:1, who in turn came to reveal the Father, John 1:18.

The Word of God, or the Bible, is actually a collection of "books," 66 in all. 39 Old Testament, or before Christ; and 27 New Testament, or from Christ to the Revelation which makes up the whole Bible. The Bible records the words of God spoken through men of God inspired by the Holy Spirit.

In II Timothy 3:16-17, we read the following: "All Scripture is inspired by God and profitable for teaching, for reproof, for correction, for training in righteousness; so that the man of God may be adequate, equipped for every good work. "

The study of God's Word, done in a systematic manner, will mold our character to become fully what God has already made us to be. Some key characteristics of the Word of God include:

- It endures (I Peter 1:25)
- It is food for the soul (Jeremiah 15:16)
- It is written on the heart (Deuteronomy 11:18)
- It furnishes light (Psalm 119:105)
- It is loved by the saints (Psalm 119:97)

- It is mighty in influence (Jeremiah 5:14, 23:29; Ezekiel 37:7; Romans 1:16; Ephesians 6:17; Hebrews 4:12)
- It purifies the life (John 17:17; Ephesians 5:26)
- It is our standard of faith (Proverbs 29:18)
- It is to be studied (Deuteronomy 17:19; Isaiah 34:16; John 5:39; Romans 15:4)
- It is absolutely trustworthy (Matthew 5:18; Ezekiel 12:25)

How Do We Study The Word Of God?

- With an attitude of reverence.
- With a desire for wisdom and understanding.
- With a desire to be changed or transformed. (Romans 12:1-2)
- With a plan for study (systematically), whether by topic, biography, or book by book.

Memorize this Scripture and hide it in your heart, Psalm 119:11.

The Word Of God Must Be:

Studied- see II Timothy 2:15.

Meditated on - see Psalm 119:148.

Acted upon- see James 1:22-23.

Where Do We Study The Word Of God?

Preferably in the same place each day and at the same time, especially first thing in the morning and just before going to bed. Carry a Bible to read while sitting and waiting for others.

Doing The Word

1. Where in the Bible have you been reading lately? Discuss what you are learning.

2. Commit with someone to read the same chapters and books, and start a discussion of the passages on a regular basis. Where would you begin and why?

3. What are your most loved and important scripture references? Present three.

For more, see *Fresh Manna*: Dr. Stan DeKoven. Vision Publishing. And "Understanding Your Bible". Ken Chant. Vision Publishing.

Chapter XI

Laying on of Hands

The first time I "laid hands on" and prayed for something or someone was shortly after I committed my life to Jesus. Our family dog had become quite ill with a tumor in the throat. You see, as a new believer, I didn't know enough "religion" to know that God doesn't heal animals. I just believed. I laid hands on my dog's head and commanded in the name of Jesus that she be healed, and she was!

I don't always know the mysteries of God, but I know that when we obey His commands, He will use us for His purposes. I have witnessed and participated in many such miracles of God, many of which have been accomplished with the laying on of hands.

Why "laying on of hands?" Laying on of hands seems no more than a ritual in the modem church. Therefore, it may be surprising that Hebrews 6:2 lists it as one of the foundational principles of the doctrine of Christ. However, as we shall see, the laying on of hands has biblical significance far beyond an empty ritual.

Let us search the Scriptures for answers to these questions about the laying on of hands.

What Is The Purpose Of Laying On Of Hands?

The laying on of hands is a means of imparting divine blessings. It signifies a transfer between two parties.

The first mention of laying on of hands in Scripture indicates its significance throughout the rest of the Bible. Genesis 48:9 records that as old Jacob was about to die, his grandsons, the sons of Joseph, were brought to his sickbed so that he might bless them. Look at Genesis 48:14. What did he do?

The purpose of this is again indicated in verse 20: *"And he blessed them that day."* However, this does not mean laying on of hands merely confers human approval, for the rest of verse 20 shows that Jacob pronounced God's blessing as he laid hands on them: "By you Israel will pronounce blessing, saying, 'May God make you like Ephraim and Manasseh!'"

The purpose of laying on of hands is also indicated by comparison of two New Testament passages. Acts 13:3 records that *"they laid their hands on"* Saul and Barnabas in the church at Antioch. The significance of this is implied in Acts 14:26, which states that Saul and Barnabas later returned"... from which they had been commended to the grace of God for the work that they had accomplished. "This indicates both a sharing in the mission and accountability to one another.

What Blessings Are Imparted By The Laying On Of Hands?

The laying on of hands can bring healing from God.

- According to Mark 6:4-5, "He laid his hands upon a few sick people and healed them."

- According to Mark 16:17-18, "... they will lay hands on the sick, and they will recover"

- Again in Acts 28:8, "... he laid his hands on him and healed him"

The laying on of hands is used to impart God's blessing on a new ministry.

- Acts 6:1-6 describes the selection of seven men by the church at Jerusalem as deacons. "And these they brought before the apostles; and after praying, they laid their hands on them."

- Acts 13:1-3 describes the sending out of Saul and Barnabas by the church at Antioch. According to verse 3, "Then, when they had fasted and prayed and laid their hands on them, they sent them away." The laying on of hands is used to impart the gift of the Holy Spirit.

The laying on of hands is used to impart the Gift of the Holy Spirit.

According to Acts 8:1-17, Peter and John, "Then they *began* laying their hands on them, and they were receiving the Holy Spirit."

According to Acts 19:6, "And when Paul had laid his hands upon them, the Holy Spirit came on them, and they *began* speaking with tongues and prophesying. "

Laying on of hands is used to impart the spiritual gifts?

- In I Timothy 4:14, Paul wrote to Timothy, "Do not neglect the spiritual gift within you, which was bestowed on you through prophetic utterance with the laying on of hands by the presbytery."

- Paul again wrote in II Timothy 1:6, "For this reason I remind you to kindle afresh the gift of God which is in you through the laying on of my hands."

The word "gift" in both of these passages is the Greek word *charisma,* which is used in the Bible elsewhere to describe spiritual gifts. See Romans 12:6; I Corinthians 12:4. The Bible uses a different word *dorea* for the gift of the Holy Spirit Himself. As Christians, we receive the Gift, the Holy Spirit. The Holy Spirit is the keeper of the gifts or manifestations of the Holy Spirit, and gives them to and through believers as He will.

Laying on of hands is to be more than a ritual in the church. Laying on of hands is used in some churches for confirmation, which can be blessing. However, the word confirm and establish, is done by encouragement, instruction and exhortation – Acts 14:22; 15:32.

Laying on of hands is sometimes used indiscriminately to impart spiritual gifts without divine revelation. The distribution of spiritual gifts is determined by the Holy Spirit. *"He gives them to each one, just as He determines,"* See I Corinthians 12:8-11.

Hands are sometimes laid on candidates for church offices without sufficient time to prove them. God's word warns against this in I Timothy 5:22.

The laying on of hands is an important, foundational principle of God's word; a blessing when used according to God's Word.

Doing The Word

1. From your view, what is the purpose of laying on of hands?

2. According to scripture, in your own words, what blessings are imparted by the laying on of hands?

3. Why is it important to use Laying on of hands to impart the spiritual gifts?

4. Do you have a special need? Do you need healing? Do you need the power of the Holy Spirit? Do you need a spiritual gift for God's work? Ask a spirit-filled man or woman to lay hands on you. Allow the Lord to use you to bless others.

Chapter XII

Resurrection of the Dead

Mrs. Maxwell was a 72-year-old woman who had lived a long and fruitful life. She had been a dear and precious woman, a soul winner and teacher of children in the Body of Christ. When she passed away, I was asked by the family to conduct the funeral.

In her family, half of her children and most of her grandchildren were Christians, but half of them were not. What a difference between the two groups.

To the Christian family members, Mrs. Maxwell's death was a time of great rejoicing. They knew that she was with her Lord. But to her children who did not know Jesus, it was a time of great fear, sorrow, and uncertainty.

One of the beautiful aspects of being born again is that we have assurance of eternal life with our Lord. Resurrection of the dead is foundational to our walk with the Lord and should be understood by all true Christians.

We live in a time when people are quite self-oriented, or narcissistic. They say, "eat, drink, and be merry, for tomorrow we die!" This point of view seems reasonable to the "present" generation, and has permeated the church as well.

God's point of view is different. In God's Word, the future is constantly held before us as an incentive for righteousness in this present world.

Two events are included in the foundational principles of the doctrine of Christ: Resurrection of the dead and Eternal judgment.

The resurrection of the dead is a blessed hope for all believers. This will be obvious as we look at the four different bodily resurrections distinguished in the Bible.

Individuals Were Temporarily Resurrected

These include the following:

- The son of the widow of Zarephath (I Kings 17:17-24).

- The son of the Shunamite woman (II Kings 4:18-37).

- A man who was thrown in Elisha's grave (II Kings 13:20-21).

- Many saints who were raised after Jesus' resurrection (Matthew 27:52-53).

- The son of the widow of Nain (Luke 7:11-18).

- Lazarus (John 11) Tabitha (Acts 9:36-43) Eutychus (Acts 20:9-12) Apparently other individuals have been raised, both in biblical times (Matthew 10:8) and in this age.

However, these resurrections have all been temporary, for I Corinthians 15:20 declares, "But now Christ has been raised from the dead, the first fruits of those who are asleep." John 5:28-29, says the resurrection of life was to happen in the future. These temporary resurrections are not part of the *"resurrection of the dead,"* which is foundational for Christians, according to Hebrews 6:2. Any resurrection of the dead before Jesus' final appearing is also temporary and a wonderful miracle!

Christ Was Resurrected

According to Luke 23:43, Christ said to the thief on the cross, "Truly I say to you, today you shall be with Me in Paradise." This referred to Christ's spirit, for verse 46 records, "And Jesus, crying out with a loud voice, said, "Father, into your hands I commit my spirit." Having said this, he breathed his last."

In contrast, the body of Jesus was buried by Joseph of Arimathea, and arose three days later (Luke 23:50-24:7). Luke 24:39 shows that the Body of Christ was raised. Jesus said, "See My hands and My feet, that it is I Myself; touch Me and see, for a spirit does not have flesh and bones as you see that I have." Those who do not believe in the resurrection of the body do not believe in the resurrection at all (I Corinthians 15:1-4).

Draw a line from each characteristic of Jesus' resurrection body to the scripture reference where it is found:

Flesh and bones	Luke 24:39
Ate food	John 20:24, 27
Could be touched	Luke 24:42-43
Had scars of the crucifixion	Luke 24:39
Appeared in a locked room	Acts 1:9
Disappeared	John 20:19, 26
Ascended	Luke 24:31

All Christianity depends on the resurrection of Christ. The apostles preached the resurrection in Acts 4:2. Look up the consequences of denial of the resurrection in I Corinthians 15:14, 17-18.

Christians Who Have Died Are Resurrected

When a believer dies, his soul goes immediately to be with the Lord.

Paul expected to go immediately into the presence of Christ when he died. Philippians 1:21, "For to me, to live is Christ and to die is gain." He is talking about death when he writes in verse 23, "But I am hard-pressed from both directions, having the desire to depart and be with Christ, for *that* is very much better."

Yet, Paul also looked for the resurrection of his body in the future, for he wrote in Philippians 3:20-21, "For our citizenship is in heaven, from which also we eagerly wait for a Savior, the· Lord Jesus Christ; who will transform the body of our humble state into conformity with the body of His glory, by the exertion of the power that He has even to subject all things to Himself."

The Unsaved Will Be Resurrected

At death, the unsaved immediately go into separation from God. Jesus told of a rich man who died and was *"in hell where he was in torment"* Luke 16:22-23. This refers to his soul, since it took place immediately at death. The place where the unsaved go at death is *hades* in Greek, translated hell in the KJV.

According to Revelation 20, the bodies of the unsaved will come out of the sea or death (the grave), and their souls will come out of hell *hades.* They will then be judged and cast into the lake of fire. Jesus used a different word, *gehenna,* for the lake of fire. Also, Gehenna was a place outside of Jerusalem where flesh was burned (Matthew 10:28). Thus, there are two places called hell - hades, where the souls of the unsaved go at death, and gehenna, where the body and soul go after the resurrection and judgment.

Doing The Word

You must believe in the bodily resurrection of Christ to be a Christian.

1. What fears do you have, if any, of the resurrection?

2. Define and discuss the meaning of Resurrection.

3. Who will be resurrected?

For more, see *When the Trumphet Sounds*: Dr. Ken Chant. Vision Publishing.

Chapter XIII

Eternal Judgment

Death will not be the end for you. What you do in this life will determine how you spend eternity. This is the doctrine of eternal judgment, named in Hebrews 6:2 as one of the foundational principles of the doctrine of Christ.

The New Testament is futuristic, using the future as an incentive for the right choices in this present life. The Bible teaches only two possible results of eternal judgment.

Let's see what the Bible says about this subject.

The Unsaved Will Be Judged With Eternal Punishment

Let us follow the destiny of an unsaved man:

At death, the unsaved go immediately to hell *(hades).* Jesus tells about such a man in Luke 16:22-24. The word translated hell is *hades,* the place of the dead. This passage refers to his soul, since his body was buried and would not suffer torment in the grave. It cannot refer to the future time of the resurrection, for he still had brothers on earth who needed to repent so they could escape punishment in hell. See verses 27-31.

The bodies of the unsaved will be resurrected to stand in judgment. Turn to Revelation 20:11-15 and look up these facts about the judgment of the unsaved.

- What was the place of the judgment (v 11)? Who were the people at the judgment? The reference is clearly speaking of both the believer in Jesus Christ and the unbeliever.

- What was the book that was to be used as a basis for judgment?

- Based upon what was found in the book they would be judged according to what?

The Result Of The Judgment

Thus, there are two hells in Scripture: *hades,* where the souls of the unsaved go after death; and the *lake of fire,* where their souls and bodies will go after judgment.

The Saved Will Be Judged For Eternal Rewards

Let us now follow the destiny of a Christian.

- At death, the Christian goes immediately into the presence of Christ. I Corinthians 5:8.

- When Christ returns, He will bring with Him the souls of dead Christians. I Thessalonians 4:14-17.

Christians Will Be Rewarded At The Judgment Seat Of Christ

II Corinthians 5:10, "For we must all appear before the judgment seat of Christ, so that each one may be recompensed for his deeds in the body, according to what he has done, whether good or bad "

Further, Christians will clearly receive different rewards, Matthew 16:27; I Corinthians 3:13-15.

The many activities by which we may receive rewards include the love we show, Matthew 25:36-46, the degree to which we fulfill our calling, Matthew 25:14-30, our commitment to God's kingdom, Matthew 6:20-24, and our endurance under persecution, Matthew 5:10-12.

The saved live and reign with Christ. Revelation 20:4-6. Hallelujah!

The Saved Will Live With God Eternally In The New Heaven And Earth

Revelation 21:2, "And I saw the holy city, new Jerusalem, coming down out of heaven from God, made ready as a bride adorned for her husband."

Doing The Word

1. You must face eternal judgment. What difference does this fact make in the life you are now living? Are you ready? If not, turn from your sins and commit yourself to Christ.

2. Discuss the differences between saved and unsaved in terms of their afterlife.

For more see "When the Trumpet Sounds". Dr. Ken Chant. Vision Publishing.

Chapter XIV

Living the Christian Life

We have seen that salvation, becoming born again, is the beginning of a new life. The Lord desires for each of us to live life to its fullest, to become all we already are in Christ. Living the Christian life effectively is something that concerns every Christian.

Our first stage in living the Christian life fully, is to develop an intimate relationship with Jesus. In this section, you will see the essentials needed to live for Jesus day by day. We all must experience this intimate dependency, developed out of obedience to His word in order to be full in Him, Hebrews 12:1.

The Christian life is likened to a race. You have to finish the course to win. Eternal security, the belief of once saved, always saved, is an assurance for true believers. It is true. However, the Bible is filled with warnings to Christians of the danger of damnation if having once experienced Jesus, they turn from Christ. The book of Hebrews especially warns of this danger.

Look at Hebrews 10:26-29. It gives a sober warning.

This does not mean that anyone who has willfully sinned can never be forgiven; that would be contrary to the rest of Scripture, James 5:19-20; I John 1:9. It means there is no sacrifice for sin if we return to the law for our salvation. Salvation is by grace through faith alone; at the same time, God does not want us to continue to sin. See Romans 6:1, 2. The New American Standard Version translates it, "What shall we say then? Are we to continue in sin so that grace may increase? 4 May it never be! How shall we who died to sin still live in it?"

We must have our hearts fully set on the grace and truth of God, not rely on our work (as the Judaizers of that day) to save or keep us. Nor should we continue to willfully sin... but seek God's strength and accountable relationships in the church to overcome our "besetting sins."

The Book of Hebrews tells how we can overcome sin and live a life of holiness. Let us look at some of the help Hebrews offers for our Christian life.

Go To Jesus When You Need Help

Hebrews 4:14-16 reads, "Therefore, since we have a great high priest who has passed through the heavens, Jesus the Son of God, let us hold fast our confession. For we do not have a high priest who cannot sympathize with our weaknesses, but One who has been tempted in all things as *we are, yet* without sin. Therefore, let us draw near with confidence to the throne of grace, so that we may receive mercy and find grace to help in time of need." Hebrews 12:2 tells us to keep our eyes fixed on Jesus.

Notice two things for which we can come to Jesus and find help.

1. We can *"obtain mercy"* when we have sinned. Do not give up if you fail! Come to Jesus in prayer and be instantly forgiven, instantly, so that you do not experience condemnation.

2. We can *"find grace to help"* overcome temptation *"time of need."*

Live By Faith In Christ

This means that faith in Christ becomes the primary motivation for our life. Just as we are saved by faith, we are continually kept by faith. See I Peter 1:5. According to Hebrews 3:12, what is it that could cause departing from God? If we were to scan Hebrews 11, we would see these great men and women of God are examples of living by faith. They simply trusted God!

See *Grace and Truth: Twin Towers of the Father's Heart:* Dr. Stan DeKoven. Vision Publishing.

Stay In Fellowship With The Church

We receive strength and encouragement from other Christians to help us live a Christian life. The church is the Body of Christ. Dropping out of the church is like cutting off one's hand. Hebrews 10:25 states; "forsake not our own assembling together, as is the habit of some, but encouraging *one another;* and all the more as you see the day drawing near."

Submit To God's Discipline

God does not cause all the troubles in our life, but He will use them for our good if we love Him and do His will, Romans 8:28; James 1:2-3. It is foolish to turn from God because trials come. That is when we need Him the most. Examine the following scriptures thoroughly to see the wisdom and care of God for us.

Whom does God discipline? Hebrews 12:6, "for those whom the Lord loves he disciplines, and he scourges every son whom he receives." What response must we give to God's discipline? See Hebrews 12:9. What is the purpose of discipline? See Hebrews 12:10.

Beware Of Bitterness

According to Hebrews 12:15, there is a type of trouble that can cause us to stumble and become defiled. "See to it that no one comes short of the grace of God; that no root of bitterness springing up causes trouble, and by it many be defiled."

Rebellion against God's appointed leaders is actually rebellion against God himself. Hebrews 13:7 exhorts, "Remember those who led you, who spoke the word of God to you; and considering the result of their conduct, imitate their faith."

God provides for us help and safety in and through His word and with the help of others in the family of God, especially our spiritual leaders.

Doing The Word

Remember, it is not enough to start the Christian life; you must finish. Just keep on keeping on. If you stumble, get up again! In what areas of your Christian walk do you need assistance? How could you improve your walk, according to what you have learned in this chapter?

As I mentioned previously, I was saved at age 12, in a small Evangelical Methodist Church in San Diego, California. My pastor, Lee Speakman was a true man of God, who laid a solid biblical foundation and example of Christian Living for me. And from that foundation, I needed to continue to grow...and so do you!

1. List and define the key elements to growing as a believer.

2. Why is fellowship so important in the Christian life?

3. Why is discipline so important in the Christian life?

For more, see *Christian Life*: Dr. Ken Chant. Vision Publishing.

Chapter XV

The Local Church

In 1970, at 17 years of age, I met my dear friend and fellow pastor, Dr. Bohac. He was my high school English teacher and an Assembly of God minister. Not only did he assist me in the Baptism of the Holy Spirit, he performed the wedding ceremony for my wife Karen and me. I also had the unique privilege of helping him restart a church in San Diego, California.

The little church (Logos Chapel) began with only ten people, which five, including me, were members of a Christian singing group.

We questioned many times, "Did we truly hear from the Lord?" Yet, we knew for certain that God's promises were true, that we were to become a strong church in the San Diego area. The Lord was gracious, and through His grace we steadily increased. I learned about church life from my pastor and my early church experiences, and have been in love with the church ever since.

The local church, especially one which has a strong vision for Christ, is essential for our Christian growth. We need to be willing to commit ourselves to the Lord and His work through the local church. Let's look at the local church and its importance. Local church means the individual congregation and the other congregations in your locality for the believer as part of the larger Body of Christ (church of the locality) in your city. But first a sobering thought.

Jesus loves his church and so must we. In spite of the dysfunctions found in some church congregations, and the foolish mistakes of some of the churches leaders, Jesus loves his church, the community of faith needed to nurture every believer.

What Is The True Church?

"Church" is translated from the Greek word *ekklesia,* which literally means "called out." Thus, the church consists of all the people whom God has called out from the world. When we are saved, we are Baptized into Christ and become a member of Christ's church. Members of various church organizations may be part of the one true church, but the church is not identified with any one organization.

Now let us search the Scriptures to identify the church as we have just described it. The church began with Christ's earthly ministry, and will continue throughout this age.

In Matthew 16:18 Jesus says, "I also say to you that you are Peter, and upon this rock I will build My church; and the gates of Hades will not overpower it"

Hades is the place of the dead, so this means that His church will endure forever. All true Christians are part of the church. See Acts 2:47 "...And the Lord was adding to their number day by day those who were being saved."

The true church is not identified by any particular name, for many names are used in Scripture, including *"church of God"* Acts 20:28; *"churches of Christ"* Romans 16:16; *"Body of Christ"* I Corinthians 12:27; *"the church of the living God"* I Timothy 3:15; *"the general assembly and church of the firstborn"* Hebrews 12:23; *"assembly"* James 2:22.

Must I Become A Member Of A Church?

Yes. You belong in a definite place within the church. Paul could write to the church in a locality and expect his letter to be delivered to a group of believers, I Corinthians 1:2; Galatians 1:2, etc. These passages show our responsibility to be part of a local church.

Paul wrote to a local church, I Corinthians 12:27, *"Now you are the Body of Christ, and each one of you is a part of it."* Just as a member of a body has a definite place, we each have a definite place in the Body of Christ.

Which Church Should I Join?

Being a part of a strong local congregation is vital to our Christian walk. There are no perfect churches, but there are biblical characteristics of a church that describe what we should be a part of and what we should not be a part of.

We should not join a church that is not true to God's Word. II Corinthians 6:14 says, "Do not be bound together with unbelievers; for what partnership have righteousness and lawlessness, or what fellowship has light with darkness?"

Our church must be one where the "new birth," born-again experience is a vital part.

We should not join a church that denies the power of God. II Timothy 3:5 warns, "holding to a form of godliness, although they have denied its power; Avoid such men as these." This includes leaders who deny miracles of the past, and any preachers who deny miracles today. See Acts 9:26.

God will give us a definite place where we can fit in and function as members of the Body of Christ. Each of us is unique and has a definite part in the ministry of a local church. See Romans 12:3-8 and I Corinthians 12:18.

Look for relationships with other believers in a particular place. See Ephesians 4:16.

How Is The Church Governed?

The entire church is subject to Christ, its head, Ephesians 1:22; Colossians 1:1. The churches appoint their leaders through the revelation of Holy Spirit through the pastoral team. The apostles instructed the congregation, Acts 6:3, "Therefore, brethren, select from among you seven men of good reputation, full of the Spirit and of wisdom, whom we may put in charge of this task." The church is governed by elders in a city. Compare Acts 20:17 and 28. In verse 17, those Paul is speaking to are called elders.

In verse 28, the same men are called overseers. In Titus 1:5 and 7, elders and bishop are used interchangeably.

Deacons serve the church, for deacon means **servant.** Read Acts 6:1-10 for the qualifications.

Local churches may cooperate in matters of common concern, such as agreement on doctrines and practices, Acts 15:1-29; pooling finances in a joint project, I Corinthians 16:1-4; setting churches in order, Titus 1:5-9.

However, there is no single government over the church other than Christ, the head of the church, who leads through His delegated authority. See Ephesians 4:11, "The Five-Fold Ministry".

What Is My Responsibility To The Church?

- We should be faithful in attendance, Acts 2:42.

- We should support our church and its leaders with tithes and offerings flowing from a heart of generosity, according to 1 Corinthians 9:14.

- We should submit to the spiritual leaders of our church. See Hebrews 13:7.

- We should serve and strengthen one another through our individual gifting. See I Peter 4:10, and Hebrews 3:15.

Doing The Word

The primary focus of the church is to win the lost, disciple people to maturity, equip and train them, and send them out to win the lost. This can occur only in the context of the local church. In becoming an active part, you too can "sow your life for something greater than yourself" expanding the Kingdom of God!

Are you committed to a local church? How could you assist the church you are in?

1. Define what the church is.

2. How does one become a member of Christ's Church?

3. Discuss your responsibility in the church. Where do you see yourself serving in the future?

See *The Church* by Barry and Dr. Ken Chant. Vision Publishing. For more, see *Building the Church God Wants*: Dr. Ken Chant. Vision Publishing. *Setting the House in Order* and *Supernatural Architecture*. Dr. Stan DeKoven. Vision Publishing.

Chapter XVI

Marriage and the Home

Marriage was originated by God. After He created the first man, God said, "Then the LORD God said, "It is not good for the man to be alone; I will make him a helper suitable for him," Genesis 2:18.

Although some individuals are called to a celibate life for God's service, Matthew 19:10-12, marriage is undoubtedly best for most people, I Corinthians 7.

God has a plan for marriage, and you need to know about it. Below is a brief outline of the biblical teaching that you can apply to your own situation.

What Is Marriage?

Biblically, we can define marriage as a covenant, binding agreement, of companionship consummated by sexual union between a man and woman. According *to* Genesis 2:18, "Then the LORD God said, "It is not good for the man to be alone; I will make him a helper suitable for him.""

Genesis 2:24 records God's description of marriage, "For this reason a man shall leave his father and his mother, and be joined to his wife; and they shall become one flesh." I Corinthians 6:16 shows that becoming one flesh refers to the sexual union.

What Are Some Violations Of *God's* Plan For Marriage?

Since God's plan is for one man and one woman to be joined together as one flesh, anything else is less of God's plan. It misses the mark. These violations may include the following:

1. Having more than one wife at a time, Genesis 4:19; Kings 11:1-4.

2. Adultery, Exodus 20:14; James 4:4.

3. Homosexual relationships, Leviticus 18:22; Romans 1:26-27.

4. Divorce, except in certain special situations where it is allowed, not mandated, i.e., adultery, abandonment, sexual immorality, Matthew 5:31-32; 19:3-9.

What Are Some Responsibilities Of Husbands And Wives To Each Other?

1. Husbands and wives are responsible to be faithful to one another. Exodus 20:14, "You shall not commit adultery"

2. Husbands and wives are responsible to love one another.

   Ephesians 5:25, "Husbands, love your wives, just as Christ also loved the church and gave Himself up for her,"

   Titus 2:4 says that older women should teach young women *"to love their husbands. "*

   Notice that married love is not an uncontrollable feeling: it is commanded and is therefore an act of the will and an attitude of the heart and mind. If nurtured, it will grow.

3. Husbands and wives are responsible to satisfy the sexual needs of one another:

   I Corinthians 7:3-5, "The husband must fulfill his duty to his wife, and likewise also the wife to her husband. The wife does not have authority over her own body, but the husband *does;* and likewise also the husband does not have authority over his own body, but the wife *does.*

   stop depriving one another, except by agreement for a time, so that you may devote yourselves to prayer, and come together again so that Satan will not tempt you because of your lack of self-control."

4. Husbands and wives are responsible to remain with one another, 1 Corinthians 7:10.

What Are The Special Responsibilities Of Husbands?

1. Husbands are commanded to love unselfishly, beyond the degree of love required of wives, Ephesians 5:2.

2. Husbands are responsible for the material support of their families, 1 Timothy 5:8.

What Are The Special Responsibilities Of Wives?

Wives are responsible to show respect to their husbands. Ephesians 23-24. This does not mean a wife must obey even if her husband orders her to do something sinful. She is to submit *"as unto the Lord,"* and the Lord never commands us to do evil.

Wives are responsible to help their husbands, wherever possible. As we have seen, when God first created woman, He said, "I will make him a helper suitable for him," Genesis 2:18.

What Does The Bible Teach About Divorce?

In general, the Bible teaches that marriage is for life, as we have already seen in Matthew 5:31-32; 19:3-9. Christ does allow for the right to divorce and remarry, in exceptional cases. Matthew 5:32.

1. Those divorcing in spite of this should remain unmarried, 1 Corinthians 7:11.

2. Those who have divorced and remarried wrongfully should not try to return to former companions, Deuteronomy 24:1-4. By remarriage, they have broken the former marriage, Mathew 19:9, and if they come to Christ, they will be forgiven, 2 Corinthians 5:17.

What Are Some Responsibilities Of Parents And Children?

1. Parents should not be overly harsh with their children. See Colossians 3:21. Parents should provide spiritual training for their children. In Ephesians 6:4, fathers are commanded to *"bring them up in the nurture and admonition of the Lord. "*

2. Children should honor their parents, Ephesians 6:1.

Doing The Word

I am most aware that this is a very brief synopsis of a Christian home. For more information see your pastor and refer to Dr. DeKoven's book *Marriage and Family Life* and *Parenting on Purpose* .

1. How well am I doing as a husband/wife?

2. If single, what changes might I need to make to insure that I am the kind of man/woman pleasing to God?

3. What are the primary responsibilities of a man toward a woman in marriage?

4. What are the primary responsibilities of a woman toward a man in marriage?

5. What does the bible teach about divorce? Do you agree?

6. What are some key responsibilities of parents to children from your perspective?

Chapter XVII

Handling Your Money

Over the past few years I have become increasingly aware of the need for money to extend the Kingdom of God. The Word of God says a great deal about money and what our attitude towards it should be. This is an important topic for the new believer.

In my counseling ministry, one of the primary stresses on individuals and couples is the inability to properly handle money. In my own family this was a primary area of conflict between my parents. There was never enough money to go around.

We serve a very practical God. He knows what we need and is concerned about every area of our lives. In this section we will examine the handling of our money from a biblical perspective. It's about the heart.

According to Jesus, your attitude toward money is the test of what kind of person you are. See Luke 16:10-11.

According to verse 9, the *"true riches"* refer to the *"eternal dwellings,"* or heaven. He further said, *"Where your treasure is, there will your heart be also,"* Matthew 6:21.

God's plan for your money is revealed throughout the Bible, but Proverbs especially covers a wide range of financial subjects. Therefore, we are going to use Proverbs as a basis for our study, along with some other passages that amplify Proverbs' teaching on money.

Learn God's Will For Your Finances

The handling of personal finances is summarized in Proverbs 30:8-9.

This warns of the danger of extremes. We should not prize poverty, which can tempt us to be dishonest or even resent God. The wisdom of this is evident when we realize the rate of crime is higher and the rate of Christianity is lower where there is abject poverty.

On the other hand, the rich face the danger of prideful self-sufficiency. Of course, God may choose that some of his people be rich, like Abraham, Genesis 13:2, or that others may suffer for his sake, like Lazarus, Luke 16:19-23. But in general, we should expect that all of our needs will be met, though not necessarily all of our wants.

Do Not Waste What God Gives You

God's word instructs us to be good stewards of all he provides us. Proverbs 18:9 says, "He also who is slack in his work is brother to him who destroys."

"When they were filled, He said to His disciples, "Gather up the leftover fragments so that nothing will be lost." John 6:12.

Proverbs 6:6 and 6:8 exhorts, "Go to the ant, O sluggard, Observe her ways and be wise."…"Prepares her food in the summer *And* gathers her provisions in the harvest."

Be Diligent In Your Work

Proverbs 21:5, "The plans of the diligent *lead* surely to advantage, but everyone who is hasty *comes* surely to poverty."

We should consider it a spiritual duty to excel in our work. Although Ephesians 6:5-8 was first addressed to slaves, they were the workers of that era, so it applies to employees of our day. Verse 8 shows that it applied to the free as well as to the slave.

Avoid Debt If Possible

Proverbs 22:7 declares, "The rich rules over the poor, And the borrower *becomes* the lender's slave."

This is as true today as in biblical times. The borrower does not fully own his possessions, for the lender has a claim to them if the debt is not paid. Further, the borrower actually works for the lender, since part of his labor goes to pay the principle and interest. Not only does the borrower have a legal obligation, he has a divine obligation. Psalms 37:21 declares, *"the wicked borrow and do not repay."*

This raises a question. Does Romans 13:8 mean all debt is wrong when it says, *"owe no man anything?"* No, this verse does not mean all debt is wrong. In context, *"owe"* in Romans 13:8 refers to a **debt that is unpaid** (past due), for the passage is teaching that Christians must meet the obligations imposed by government (verses 1-7). The preceding verse 7 says, *"Give everyone what you owe him."* So debt is generally undesirable, but not totally prohibited.

Do Not Guarantee Debts For Others

Proverbs 22:26 warns, "Do not be among those who give pledges. Among those who become guarantors for debts." This often causes hard feelings as well as financial loss. Do not rescue someone, for dependency on you instead of on God might develop.

Share Your Goods With The Needy

Proverbs 19:17, "One who is gracious to a poor man lends to the LORD, And He will repay him for his good deed." Proverbs 21:13, "He who shuts his ear to the cry of the poor. Will also cry himself and not be answered"

Give To God

Proverbs 3:9-10, "Honor the LORD from your wealth. And from the first of all your produce; So your barns will be filled with plenty. And your vats will overflow with new wine."

This verse summarizes the teaching on giving throughout the Bible: give to God even before your own needs, and God will supply your needs. Jesus said, "Give and it will be given to you. They will pour into your lap a good measure-pressed down, shaken together, *and* running over. For by your standard of measure it will be measured to you in return," Luke 6:38.

The minimal amount of giving is established throughout the Bible as a tithe, or tenth.

1. Tithing was taught before the Law of Moses, for both Abraham and Jacob tithed (Genesis 14:20; 28:22).

2. Tithing was commanded in the Law, Leviticus 27:30-34.

3. Tithing was referred to by Jesus after the Law, Matthew 23:23.

Be Generous

Paul stated in II Corinthians 9:6 *"...He who sows sparingly will also reap sparingly but he who sows bountifully will also reap bountifully."* Be generous, plan ahead.

Doing The Word

Following God's Word will help straighten out your financial affairs as well as other areas of your life.

1. What areas of your financial life have you managed well/mismanaged? Repent of your past failures, and determine to follow completely God's will for your finances.

2. Summarize from the book, the key elements to a healthy financial life.

For more see, *Financial Integrity*: Dr. Stan DeKoven and Dr. Steve Mills. Vision Publishing.

The Next Step

Now that your foundation has been laid, it is time to go deep. It is God's desire to conform us to the image of Christ. In order to have our character transformed, our minds must be renewed. This is not an event, but a process.

In order to assist the disciple and discipler to continue on their journey to wholeness, the book and study guide *40 Days to the Promise: A Way Through the Wilderness* was written. This dynamic book and journal will take you deeper into God's Word as you learn the revelations of God's transforming power. The book and guide are also available from Vision Publishing (see Bibliography).

To order, go to www.booksbyvision.com and search for the title of your book. There you will find a short description, add the book to your cart and pay with nearly any form of payment.

Recommended Reading

Chapter I

Miracle Evangelism. John Ezekiel. Powerhouse Publishing.

Strategies for Spiritual Harvest. Pat Hulsey. Harvestime International.

Chapter II

Dynamic Christian Foundations. Ken Chant. Vision Publishing.

Chapter III

40 Days to the Promise. Stan DeKoven. Vision Publishing.

Chapter IV

Faith Dynamics. Ken Chant. Vision Publishing.

Chapter V

The Church Triumphant. Dr. Ken Chant. Vision Publishing.

Chapter VI

Clothed With Power. Ken Chant. Vision Publishing.

Chapter VII

Fruit, More Fruit, Much Fruit. Eugene Smith. Vision Publishing.

Chapter VIII

Redemption: The Foundation of Worship. Dr. Michael Elliott. Vision Publishing.

Chapter IX

Prayer Power. Dr. Stan DeKoven and Dr. John Delgado. Vision Publishing.

Chapter X

Fresh Manna. Stan DeKoven. Vision Publishing.

Understanding Your Bible. Ken Chant. Vision Publishing.

Chapter XII

When the Trumpet Sounds. Ken Chant. Vision Publishing.

Chapter XIII

When the Trumpet Sounds. Ken Chant. Vision Publishing.

Chapter XIV

Grace and Truth: Twin Towers of the Father's Heart. Dr. Stan DeKoven. Vision Publishing

Christian Life. Ken Chant. Vision Publishing.

Chapter XV

The Church. Barry and Ken Chant. Vision Publishing. *Building the Church God Wants.* Ken Chant. Vision Publishing.

Supernatural Architecture and *Setting the House in Order.* Dr. Stan DeKoven. Vision Publishing.

Chapter XVI

Marriage and Family Life. Stan DeKoven. Vision Publishing.

Parenting on Purpose. Stan DeKoven. Vision Publishing.

Chapter XVII

Financial Integrity. Dr. Stan DeKoven and Dr. Steve Mills. Vision Publishing.

To order any or all of these books, see www.booksbyvision.com.

The Teaching Ministry of
Dr. Stan DeKoven

Dr. Stan DeKoven is a licensed Marriage and Family Therapist, a Creative Life Coach and consults with individuals and churches nationally and internationally. Please visit his website for a complete list of books and seminars or you may contact him at:

Dr. Stan DeKoven, President
Vision International University /Walk in Wisdom Ministries
1115 D Street
Ramona, CA. 92065
1-800-9-VISION
www.booksbyvision.com www.drstandekoven.com